Untouchable
C l o u d s

Untouchable Clouds

poems by
Lightning Brown

preface by
Reynolds Price

St. Andrews College Press
1 9 9 7

Printed by Atwood Printing Co., Inc.
in Asheville, North Carolina

For St. Andrews College Press
1700 Dogwood Mile
Laurinburg, NC 28352

ISBN: 1-879934-50-7

First Printing: July 1997

Lightning Himself

by Reynolds Price

I met Lightning Brown in the late 1970s shortly after he came to Chapel Hill from prior haunts—his birthplace in Virginia, his family home in California, his alma mater at the University of Oregon and the scene of his graduate studies, which was Germany. I was visiting a mutual friend on a summer-becalmed Rosemary Street, the calm was suddenly torn by the roar of a full-sized motorcycle, my friend said "It's Lightning!"; and I thought he meant the thing itself—Jove's thunderbolt. But then my friend rose, went to the back door and beckoned me to follow. There in the backyard dismounting from a black motorcycle was a young man of elegant and keenly focused looks. He was wearing a blood-red shirt.

And he seemed to be in his late twenties, dark haired, dark eyed with the Mediterranean air of so many Americans who derive like him from British Celtic stock. The Celts of Britain, never forget, were in intimate contact with Roman imperial soldiers for many centuries; and the streets of Swansea, Edinburgh and Belfast still display Roman genes in many a swarthy face and form, the legacy of long fraternization. Though I would later learn how profoundly Lightning had been shaped and ethically endowed by his Roman Catholic rearing, my first strong memory is of his blunt Italic grace and power, his high outrageous Celtic laughter and his love of all the spectacles of human folly—spectacles as visible in Chapel Hill as in any other village or metropolis. We may have spent an hour together that first day; and when I eventually asked what he did, he said "I'm a troublemaker. And a poet." I may have laughed a little; but years later, I'd know that he merely told the truth. He was both, in eminently useful ways; and he lived to prove it.

After that first meeting, through the crowded years

of two separate lives in the same community, We encountered each other at poetry readings, political rallies and on the sidewalks. In those days I was still walking upright, and Lightning was a few inches shorter than I. So from those early years, I recall him mainly as a man who seemed markedly younger than myself, always charged with an eager pony's vitality and always claiming he'd call me soon and arrange to meet for a drink and a talk. The claim was long delayed. In the meanwhile I was seeing occasional short poems of his in the Chapel Hill paper, mostly fairly loosely written and prosy comments on local events or the turn of a season. They seemed generally likable but seldom quite finished. I didn't know that those public poems were only the tip of a much larger mass, the dead-serious poems he'd written since high school at least. It would be many years—and all but too late—before I learned of Lightning's most passionate life's work.

Meanwhile through the years I learned various other facts about him. Supporting himself with work at the University's computer center, he'd abandoned his graduate studies in literature and was pursuing and successfully completing a law degree. He'd become deeply involved in various environmental and human rights causes. In the course of those fights, at a time when it was literally dangerous to do so, he'd candidly declared his own homosexuality. Then in the mid-eighties I was compelled to disappear from local view to manage a personal battle with cancer, and I lost all direct touch with Lightning.

In the fall of 1994, however, I arrived at the Orange County Friends School to participate in a book fair. I'd been asked to read from my work for half an hour; and when I rolled out before the gathered listeners, I saw on my left a gauntly thin, white-haired and white-bearded man. It had been so long since I'd seen Lightning Brown that I didn't recognize him, despite his wearing a black sweatshirt with a blazing lightning bolt on the chest. But after I'd signed a few books for holiday shoppers, I returned home to find my telephone ringing. "It's Lightning," he said. "I was there just now." When I asked why he hadn't come up to speak afterward, he said "I didn't know how long I could wait."

I thought I heard an ominous note, but I couldn't be sure till he came to my door a few days later for that long-postponed drink. In the years since I'd seen him, he'd lost maybe thirty pounds; and his Italo-Celtic skin had darkened further. But with the white beard and the close-cropped white head, he looked more graceful in his power than ever—a Spanish hidalgo or conquistador of endless craft and resource and still-ready laughter. Within half an hour though, he'd let me know that he'd contracted our time's dread plague—AIDS—and that his T-cell count was presently at an awful low of eight (a normal count is in the vicinity of a thousand). He said "When it goes below ten T-cells, you get to name them." I concealed my sad shock and, in a few moments, we were off and inventing ten appropriate names. As I recall, we leaned heavily on the names of Disney's Seven Dwarfs—Sleepy, Dopey, Sneezy, Grumpy, Doc and so on.

Lightning's uniquely buccaneer brand of courage marked the whole next year of our friendship. For in the place prepared by a long acquaintanceship, Lightning now demanded—and I was glad to offer—a hard-working friendship. I think it's accurate to say that I saw more of him in that last year than anyone else until near the end. Then in the summer, fall and winter of 1995-96—as his now desperate needs surpassed my own abilities to give—his family began to come from the West Coast and elsewhere and tend his dying with a valiant loving delicacy that remains unparalleled in my memory of similar crises. In the light of their continuous care, I went on seeing Lightning till the end.

Two things, I think, produced the intensity and delight of that final friendship which Lightning insisted that we forge. The first was my own decade of paraplegia and my permanent residence in a wheelchair. By late '94 Lightning was growing visibly weaker and frailer, and I think he perhaps half-consciously realized that another physically impaired person might make an easier friend than the hosts of the unthinkingly superior able-bodied whom he knew in central North Carolina and elsewhere. Second, surely—and the results on display here prove it—was the fact that, facing death, Lightning was beginning to feel the burgeoning in him of a large final efflorescence of poetry; and he wanted to share that richness with someone who was at least a craftsman in the same trade, someone who might help him bring that harvest to a wider share of the always limited audience for dead-earnest poetry.

For a whole year then—in frequent meetings and even more often on E-mail—Lightning showed me the remarkable poems that were streaming from him with unprecedented haste, volume, originality and depth. In return I'd show him new poems of my own that were surely hurried on their way toward me by Lightning's literally burning example. A number of my own simultaneous poems discussed aspects of Lightning's inexorable decline, matters that he and I freely discussed at all times; and while I initially hesitated to let him see my sadder reflections, once I'd done so I heard him respond with the lawyerly cool involvement that were a chief feature of his final months. I was, for instance, just opposite him in my room one evening when he read a poem of mine that risked a guess at the inevitable nearness of his death. When he'd read the final lines, he looked up and faced me with the unaltered grin that was always his banner; and he said "Not yet!" In other less bleak poems I speculated about the sources of our renewed friendship, and those poems he read with generous praise and thanks.

Awed by the very nature of the final torrent of poems he wrote—or received as inexplicable transmissions—he spent almost no time in revising the lines after their rushing arrival. With his already damaged vision, he'd slowly drive the eight miles to my house with a fresh manuscript, we'd sit on my deck above the small pond and he'd wait impatiently while I read that morning's poem. Eventually I'd point to a phrase or an image which had stumped me in its extreme compression or which seemed repetitive. Lightning would take a quick look over my shoulder; then he'd invariably respond "Well, that's how I *want* it." And that would be it. At that point I always retired from the fray, unwilling to risk a shut-down of our communication or of his ongoing and plainly brittle receptivity. If thirty-odd years of working with young writers had taught me anything, it had warned me of the danger of stemming a genuine flood in progress—not to mention a flood that seemed so sure to be literally autumnal, the brief high prelude to an ending.

Within a few weeks of watching Lightning's sudden outpour of poems, I asked if he'd join me in teaching a class in the coming semester at Duke. It was to be an undergraduate seminar in the Gospels of Mark and John, and it occurred to me that—now that he'd been compelled to cease to practice law—he could join us as class poet and add the nourishing complex brew of his present work to our explorations into two ancient documents that had never ceased being central to our culture and our lives. He at once accepted my invitation, specifying from the start that he'd write poems arising from our actual readings in the life of Jesus.

Despite his continued loss of strength, Lightning made it to most of the semester's classes. A friendly campus policeman always saved him a parking place within walking distance of my classroom. Since he was of no physical danger to anyone—though psychically he was still a "troublemaker" in the word's best sense—he and I silently decided not to inform the class of his illness unless they inquired. I think we both assumed that they could see the effects of the vortex he was in; and his uncompromising, laughing honesty quickly won the students' affection and respect—he seemed to them, above all, *trustworthy.*

At once the salt of his razor-sharp perceptions and the probing questions he directed at our texts made him a superb contributor and guide. And the poems he produced in response to the healings and teachings of Jesus were invariably richer than the class could digest in a single reading; yet all the students and I left the course (after a final class dinner party which Lightning managed to attend) with a sheaf of striking work by a man who was speaking from the core of a fire that consumes us all, some of us more slowly than Lightning.

With only a few exceptions those gospel poems were Lightning's last. By the early summer of '95, the virus was roaring almost audibly in him; and by August he'd entered the final tunnel of irresistible depredation that is by far the plague's cruelest assault. He and I continued to meet two or three times weekly, at my house mostly, so long as he could drive (I don't drive at all). I continued to show him new poems of my own; he always responded warmly and keenly, but his own flood was stemmed. He accepted that closure, as he had all the others, with a flawless sober dignity that would have been astounding in a seven-foot-tall ancient warrior-monarch, not to speak of a mid-sized American fighter for the poor and deprived.

And in his last weeks in the surpassingly peaceful and welcoming AIDS house in Carrboro, accompanied by his family and his nearest friends, he wrote the brief final poems of his life. In their pain they stand at the limits of our ability to bear human feeling at its nakedest. In their outrageously brave calm wit, they are utterly characteristic of their poet. So they stand in a place of earned honor at the end of this selection from the years of work which Lightning Brown left. At our final meeting four days before his death at the early age of forty-eight, I told him simply that his poems would be published. By then I could not be sure he still recognized me, but he simply said "Good." His friend Walter Bennett had made the same promise that same week, and Walter has made the greater effort to keep our vow and to see so many strong new poems available at last to the wider audience for which Lightning longed. It's a very sizable gift to us all that he wrote them, that he saved them through terrible trials and sent them on toward us as urgent news from the midst of a life that he knew to be matchless and nowhere more so than in the bare lines and the calm serenity of his last days and hours.

—17 February 1997

Contents

The Blessed Table

Always, the gods ate: snacks of nectar, grapes and
    cups of wine,
For pleasure, since they actually had no bodies that
    needed anything.
And so glory, as we might imagine it, always seems
    a banquet,
And pleasure is near where glory lodges. Does this
    make you hungry?
Then hunger and watch. You'll see them then,
    chewing our reality
Like salad. We, our daily bread the object of our
    prayers, taste
As we can, dodging the grinding surfaces of life,
    trying to eat us.

We no longer know if our gods have bodies,
    though Jesus bleeds
In cataracts along his cross of sufferings, undiagnosed.
And our bodies permeate us so deeply that death is
    a possibility,
Entire death: Such an unimaginable improbability!
    We may never know it.
And yet we, too, enjoy feasting—and must do so, if
    we are not
To be ground down ourselves. Is this godlike? No,
    but they are the immortals.
And we, we do not know whether immortality is,
    or even where to ask.

But imagine still they are before you, in brilliant colors
That make your daylights shadow, and so big their
    graceful movements:
Everything our bodies, our complicated psyches,
    were ever made to be.
Imagine them: perfections of the man and woman,

of all the many types
Of which gods may be made, even, perhaps, our
    own. Where is the difference?
Is it blasphemy to wonder if they are not our
    ancestors, and that we live
To be deity, and already are? But we are children,
    blind ants in darkness.

Still, nothing stops our imagining, nor stops our travesties
Which may be the querying and enactment of their
    truth: supple,
Above all, I imagine them, with glowing skins and
    hair like adamant;
And, silent in their speaking across negligible space,
    vivid in thought,
Our chaos a clarity transparent to their minds; and
    sometimes caring.
To see them is to worship them. It is our nature to
    love and serve the good.
How can we, divine children, have ever come so
    mortal? Knowing that,

We would then be guests, somehow, at the table
    itself, the blessed table,
And would mingle with them in the proximity of
    touch and whisperings,
And be whole of body and limitless of mind as our
    dear, living perfected selves.
What a party that would be, with them and us,
    imperceiving any removing degree
Toward our true parents, those absolute clouds of
    godhead, and their figures.
Sitting and feasting on very life without poisoning
    ourselves, immortal,
Too, proofs of the divine powers, glowing and,
    above all, supple.

Numbers

Four before three, one black, one red: imperfect hierarchy.
The random dance of aught with king, exactly
    equalling odds by freedom.
What is to win, to lose? Just feelings, even artificial?

Or what? Calculable points off a mean average, against
    probability;
the cards know what I don't, what deal–what king,
    what suit, what win, or not.

The cards. No display of scoring, just surfaced neurality
    of moves and matches,
pretending family, or seeking, or making, or given.
Life's a play, even solitaire. A speculative disparity, up
    and down:
always an ace with only one connection, flirting, booty-
    eyed
With beauty beyond the 1-2-3, in parties of disorder.
There's emptiness, glancing as if he really had a face,
as if this really were a mirror. And there my own ideal
    self, just passing.

Fool's Foot Guide

This is the condition of our new world,
our jungle-fever. Like the food of souls,
seed of sons who once may see the gods:
Light hits us. We black out.

Two hundred years deep within this continent,
oh my tender town, beloved!
Grandpa thinks like father, too,
his son has gone too far and must be dead.

Like father, so this son prays with muscle,
clambering foothills of a distant present,
making maps of years stumbled lifetimes backward,
thoughtless step for step, vagrant of warm instants.

The messenger speaks flame; our life slips around
backwards to nothing. And suddenly, the corner's turned,
and ahead, dim, we home on earthglow unimagined—
facefuls beaming from our sainted faces.

Last of the Chapel Hill Troublemakers

Admittedly, even the poor pay a high price of admission.
We are not guilty of failing to pour our riches on
The homeless, who may walk our streets with relative
  freedom
Or, better, house within the old center of our
  government policing.

Who could not be happy? Yet our residents cringe
Before hooligans at the gates, breaking and entering.
Crime has no advocate, but there is debate of laws;
The Ralphs know many answers, oracular guardians.

All I want is poetry on every of five pages in five papers;
All I want is to live here til I die, should I ever die
In this electric air, stinking of youth and of old age.
That is all I want, high as the price may be.

Someone's six-door limousine cruises by the woods
  cabin, black Cadillac.
We didn't used to see those here, but now they are
  invading
And come to tend their investments like armored shep
  herds.
Where they go from here, I will not wager. Up to
  breakfast?

Up to feast with bureaucrats, discreetly? Yes, there are
Not jobs enough to keep the wages low, and calling in
  the woods
Makes work. It could make betterment. But what a
  sacrifice,
Even of someone else's properties! Will a sidewalk repay
  this?

My woods were once an encampment for those
    homeless guys,
Who even, it is said, started fires on evenings in the
    Spring,
When there was just not enough warmth without them;
    they spread,
And Horst and the fire department had to save the woods.

There was hard, invisible work of years in making our
    wild nature.
Too, that was investment which must be respected and
    thanked
If we are to call ourselves a municipal culture, not just
    business.
Thanks for the paintings which adorned our public
    walls this year.

May there be more, and poems and plays, and sculptures
    on our public
Lawns and monuments, and beautiful zoning over every
    inch
Of what once was mere dirt, taking care of itself,
    Southern heaven.
Life forever! Even for our homeboys and homeless boys,
    a citizenship.

Atom Babies at Ground Zero

The leper boys on the sand-
stone steps, white and rosy. It is
a circus for the people, showing
their babies at the national museum,
clowning in the sun of government
memorials, the polluted reflecting pools.

Such a thieves' carnival, such a show
of wares, such a time! Processions of
burghers overflow the gates, and riches spill:
coins for the leper boys, fed from the parade.
We blot the snapshots, interrupt the wasting;
at home, the burgher winces for his empty pockets.

Being in Africa

I see your eyes now on the chill of wooded sky, lights
   like shadows in my own eyes' twilight.
Do these branches only seem to be prayers,
   stretched unceasing with every bud for light
   until they flower?
The trees eye me, and there are three crows
   malingering without much talk,
   waiting for excitement, dark and easy.
I will watch for your eyes until I see them.
   The crows gossip complacently.

   Your jungles thick with a chorus of news;
   a tropic beetle I have never seen
   whispers phosphorescent, shy to find you;
   caws of brilliant birds of paradise
   and bleats of tiny frogs bring from so far
   the crows' good-humored joke
   about a man gazing in the woods.

   The air bursts, split wide,
   surrendering to the mountain's longing for heaven,
   as the ground thunders my sigh
   and the blossoms crowd, questioning.

Watch the sky.

Mr. Magic Kuby-Brown

He never grew past two, and is now an old dog
Somewhere in New York City, where dogs are men
And some few humans smile and reach to greet him.

Those were the days, running in Chatham county,
A mega-lord of squirrels, and with mates for miles!
Such must be the dreams that entertain you still.

With all your impatient barking to make friends
With every irritated passer-by along the road,
Misunderstanding the social right to be alone,

Stupidly innocent of the threat you sometimes posed.
What confusion and sadness, a terminal two-year-old,
Ignorant of maps, and knowing only separate islands

Unjoined by any path, and without escape.

Lazarus in the Kitchen

Lord God, Creator of the dented canteloupe,
Of pork chops gray around the edges, how You feed
Your diligent poor, rich in dead vegetables
And discounted meats, in day-old bakery fresh as sky!

The movable bound of life and death, which You
      command,
Between first-quality at its starving price, and second—,
Wrapped to hide its weakening spots, politely:
We do not hunger when we buy Grade B, in faith.

Yet there was a man, whose farms produced such
      bumper crops
That spoilage would have been the harvest–til he burnt
His barns and ordered giant warehouses constructed
To hoard the surplus: then he died, not needing meat or
      drink.

We learn from his example, dining light and saucing
      without greed;
We are the resurrection of his excess, oh, so merry.
We thank you humbly, now, for all our parsimonious
      plenty,
Recognizing that life does not always glisten, though it
      feeds.

When Lazarus lay four days inside the tomb, his Savior
      came
In tears, unavoidably behind schedule. They thought
      the corpse
Would stink; but no–'twas not a corpse but Lazarus,
      shaking hands
And smiling, for a second birthday party. So my
      eggplant,

10

My tomatoes, chicken livers, cinnamon bread and well-
   trimmed cheeses:
Their nourishing fragrances waft from my refrigerator,
Awaiting their resurrections, their sautéed glories,
And answering the touches of their imperfect chef with
   blessings.

Washing with the Wine

Big jugs, basins full of precious water, retained memory
Of rainstorms in their desert. Homeliness of washing,
Luxury of hygiene as a standard for the people, a custom
More intimate than the scriptures on the doorpost:

And plenty of it, this flood of cleansing water,
For this is a high moment, a prosperous marriage,
      relatively.
But prosperous in water, not in wine, prosperous in
      visitors,
And less in lardering. Since when must guests provide?

Why would a mother care, if celebrants embarrass
For lack of drinks to give the thirsty, uninvited crowd?
But you are yourself uninvited, and they are her friends.
There must be some sign of gratitude, some blessing

Even if you do not claim to be the rabbi, the messiah.
And this trick is even a little funny, a party prank
That makes anniversary telling through the family's
      long life:
Suddenly the footbaths overflow with claret. What has
      happened?

This trick requires accomplices, so the servants know
      who did it,
But they do not pose a crisis, merely go on serving,
Guaranteed their share in the excess. And all suddenly
      believe
That even the poorest wedding may be a banquet of
      celebration.

And your family knows, as they always have suspected
And, part in fear amid the joy, want to get away before

Their generosity is caught, for which they have no
    explanation.
Will you embarrass them with your wizard joking? Why
    rock the boat?

They want to leave the party. They are already in the yard.
They send to tell you to contain your socializing and come
Away to the next stop in their travels. Who are my
    brothers?
Is not this joyful gathering your family better? But you go.

And then in Capernaum you reconnoitre with these
    brothers,
Silently mostly, through oblique asides, not knowing
    what to say,
Sons of a mother steeped in secrets and wonders, bounden
To the secrets, terrified of saying that something's the
    matter.

What will become of you, and of your brothers, and
    your mother?
And where is your father? And who are you, unknown
    man?
Suspecting only yourself, full of your own secrets,
    laughing
And shaking hands all round, containing your
    announcements

For the sake of the moment, of others' respectable
    joining.

Road Poem 3

The stars are so huge tonight, driving the freeway
After dancing the bar closed; the Dipper not called
Big for whim, but a huge reality, a plow handle
For gods to plant history, a drinking gourd pouring
Seas of light, free for quaffing. My hand's on it,
Pulling maybe north, maybe straight toward Arcturus.

Vast little highway, full of life in the middle of night;
Hardly any traffic, but an unimaginable pileup of
    galaxies,
Safe for us mortals cruising over concrete, and for the rest,
Well, even the biggest of stars have their little mysteries.
I'm not sure where we're heading, where home is, but you
Remind me, beloved steersman, rocking along in my
    speeding bark.

Eve

You, my Eve, made of my rib; meathook boy,
I am hung up on you, your potion of good and evil.
What sword bars our paradise together, richness
Of feasting, naked warmth amid humidest caresses?
Only apples now our feasting, quotidian miracles,
sweet, plain, red and never golden.
            And we stand, looking outward
Toward islands of hope, over seas of danger,
Made explorers by a memory of perfection
Or by a lack, a wanting to be grasped and taken;
While at our backs infinity blazes.

Another Rose

Smudgy erasure,
dead rose, overstayed
its visit, fade
absorbing more light
than petals reflected.

Such fools as
actually value change,
meaning eternity
to be novel
like almost whiteness.

Moment of Death

This is the way the year ends, not with a whimper
Even, but in silence and darkness abysmally profound
So that I must light a candle even to see my continuance.

So many times I have survived it, the sadness of new years,
The tragedy of time, destroyer, maker of never-
    returning pasts.
And now how I long to escape it, to climb outside the
    clocks;

Though it was a fine year, now inspected and certified,
A gift of life, of suns blooming like daily roses,
Of darknesses rivalled by those of the farthest Antipode.

Will you sit with me now, as time expires, as possibility
Invades a new cycle, suddenly fecund, cascading processes;
And we will step forward, though sitting immobile only,

Two alonenesses related, at least, by the calendar—
Adam and Steve, father-mothers together, both bearing
The baby year, both wishing for the bright old man in
    darkness,

Both loving our virgin youths, our slimy imaginations,
Our words, concretized in life's image, our ripening on
    each other.
This is the time, finally, to be born and burn

Like the flame of the candle, flickering and consuming.

Bad News

for Jackson Pollock

It is meant for us
(unnamed and growing)
to root here with the trees:

The dotted air, pink
with springtime clouds
bathes us to make flowers

invisible through time.
Oh to believe the evidence
only of expected bitterness
for today, meager February—

catastrophe the wrecked Winter news;
I believe nothing of it.
I know that when the frigid sun
sets pink, that blossoms set.

Michael

Talk is never cheap—
the listener must pay with friendly counsel,
rendering effort, or guilt.
My words are no worthier.
I tell you that growth
costs pain and time; but
my concern for you is nothing
except escape from the dull dissatisfaction
of all these years and changes
that have left me nowhere
further than this sadness.

I can write you about kisses—
writing's free and pen and paper cheap.
About kisses there is much to say,
though it is hard for us even to touch hands,
even to hug as others innocently may.
So much are we brothers that the thought is incest.

Our faces bear disfigurement, brands of fealty.
At times, scars of unfreedom are all we see,
looking at each other between joy and brimming tears.
From this myopic distance I ken only
that some light reflects
in the inaccessible memory of our eyes.

Rick Tupelo Comes to Visit

My quilt, my peaceful bed,
a daily battlefront. Enemies
garrisoned atop my desk,
embattled armies of lovers
and would-be lovers dying
to learn to survive learning

Love, invisible secret!
Hiding, eternity born yesterday,
rose, pink in its latest fadings!
Sometimes we are still born so old;
Sometimes we are never born at all;

Sometimes in my room the air
flowers gay as a garden, as
a temple of deep woods and moonlight.

Roommate

Every act of hiding was
an epiphany of imperfection.
A victim of rumors, I
confirm them doubled;
vacant, confused,
disbelieving the good that slips
unmastered by the paltry will
to gild it.

My life of unswept floors,
of dust gathered daily
only by the blind eye
half-turned dreaming.

So unquiet, so intent to hear
and then so forgetting
of all but unspoken words.

Postcard to Buddha

In your dimension our wild thoughts
are visible, little varmints
that hold your gaze, then scamper
out of sight. Here there is light,
and shadow in between the days;
sometimes I'm dreaming, some arun.

Basket

I am a beggar basket, though
I don't hold much nor long. See,
I am not empty,
and I have that dignity
made long ago by hands,
though dust grows daily
on my spots, and my weaving's
mashed and tattered.

I am my master's other palm,
who sits beside me fiddling
his tunes to passers-by,
his modest, wretched need outstretched
and wreathed with music,
though I only know the words.

Spring at Midnight

i.

As I worry over paper, outside, the flowering weeds
demonstrate their point, thinking nothing at all.
You will see some argument in this:
Lettered eyes are will-less against whatever words
find them, like blossoms opening to the touch of sunlight,
parsing their colors, specious globes of memory
which hold no flowers and no words.

Not words, but a palpable repetition, motion
of the season's admonishing green fingers:
cultivation, indisputable cycle of opening
and seed, buried off into darkness.

ii.

On some neighbor's door there is knocking.
I hear the latch and turn my ear:
an ant-explorer finds the Ozymandias
of finished sweets on a tinfoil plate,
miming invasion of lost tombs.

Bared by free and fragrant breezes,
sleepless phalanxes of Honeysuckle wake with me.
Ignorant of dreams, their night is short,
and they die without hesitation, silent expirations
of their precious breaths into rumors of dew.

iii.

I could sleep
beneath your curled

hand like a sprout,
held moist in
the dark rain—
gluttoned
from leaves presumed
dead all winter,
nourished by shady touches
close against my grown body of dreams.
I remember my shape
like colorless furled petals,
innocent of too much summer.

Cocteau and Whitman Meet in Heaven

The pastry does not sell;
rats from the fields eat it
before the customer has made his choice.
They claim to drink more beer here
than anywhere. But, the thinner the blood
in their veins, the less they remember
what anywhere was like. Pouring out
their native language, they arrange the details
of chaos without touching them ever.

How the academic fathers grimace with desire to poke;
a curly head–just so–they twitch the lips
and take air. Gasps that fall flat before open eyes.
But so much meat and concentration, mothers' breath
untouchable as a cloud of holiness around this life.
Such care for the corpses, lanced on strangers' silence.

Dirge for Our Unborn Children

Stillborn untouchables, pitiably misrouted here,
into this eccentric sphere of thin perfections,
unfit and forgotten, sinful concrescences
of wrong and mediocrity, slinking, hiding,
sparing even executioners your shame.

Monstrous and contagious, smothered memories
untranslatable as a repeating dream too
sweet or awful to live on to morning,
you amputations, fruit of our loins,
human mud, passed, remolded, passed.

Like feeble burning, mildewed fragments
of old letters, scraps glimmering out
of context, little warm enough
against this cold Autumn. Lost lifetimes,
pray for us you may be born alive.

Panic

for William Burroughs

A single night in
the long richness of his caravans.

The Patriarch is naked, the desert
cold as waves.
He waits, shivering without a moon.

Familiar as his own nakedness in the dark,
A shadow's hand brushes his thigh.
A challenge of death. Jacob dreamed.

A shadow's eyes searched his Patriarch's skin
Nothing one could grasp
His breath arrested like the split of midnight
with each breath

It was on him. He flayed against the dream
of its touch. Respectless touch against the high body
on which slaves feared the merest glance

No moon came. No time moved on his bareness
He was the moon, choking on uncanny shadow
Even his name was lost to this stranger.

But as the dawn inches to save him
and he staggers, broken body with
its new name of visions,
Israel remembers only a ghost hand's stroke
soft in the hollow of his crippled thigh.

28

Christmas, America

Year's end and now the surplus shared
Of the accounted plunder, summed and sold:
Amidst our endless many overflow
A meted joy to each according need,
Generous leftovers clutched into a feast.

The starving season's gift, a tiny truce
As inventoried wants line up for sale;
A lost sun crying to the cold
In night of wishes stolen and received.

Debts, blessings, judgments come around
With open palms, upholding or reprieved.
The end returns to cross our way again,
Lugging full sacks of hope and such,
Older than old, still begging to begin.

A Dialectic for Jeff

Every thought edges no-thought; logic is the science
Of these edges. Strange to nature's chemistry
Of imperfections, even time is bent, we're told.
Logic cuts clean to two dimensions the infinite
Modulations of any thought, edges shaped
Like the blinding future.

Suppose instead a conversation—we disagree;
The issue is unimportant, a mere matter of focus
On the line we draw to cut our opposite sides.
Suppose, for example, Columbus, sailing across
A boundary of thought, criminal ship
Borne on a mania tide of rumor.
Where no-thought makes its edge with reason,
Sirens are born. Form the opposite world,
History's bend suddenly transforms maps;
Parades of wildmen cross the land,
Questionably tamed curiosities conquering
(Behemoths roving maddened after the unthought,
Monstrous horsemen from the sea, poxed,
Hideously two-dimensional); wars break out against the
    unease
Of new worlds; contradictions spawn endlessly.

Columbuses after the fact, we await arrival in the
    Hollywood
Mapped with stars' homes and images of public dreams,
    never
Yet quite present in the flesh. Never have we explored
    past the edge,
And the titanic collisions of old worlds has yet to
    squeeze out
The saving commonplace, the seed, brought home from
    the tropics,
Which may blossom and bear new universes.

30

Winter Solstice

The tide of mother water,
like tropic wind borrowing heat,
upwards underwater rain, does not know,
rippling, your aureole around you,
will not know for weeks yet,
fanning hot your fantasy of
weeks of starfish reaching.
As if worth of landscape made seasons:
Summer is this instant at its peak.

Distance, starfish skeleton buried
in deepest dark, blackness of volcanic sand,
paradox of Alaskan midnight, deep-
frozen memory of the highest beaches.

Vampire Warning

Open your deskbook to the compound interest tables.
You will see how time makes its return, now this little,
Soon an overflow from a field fed on richest blood.
One bite, and then, one day, the whole town's out for
    dinner.
You may see it, flecking the fervid smiles and burning gazes,
Slightly pinkish, of the fascinating stranger, friend or
    neighbor.

Take my warning, if it is not already now too late for you:
Your love may be hazardous. A hunger, a need for
    others' warmth
Could be your symptoms—Are you run down, chasing
    others' blessing?
Do you cook grand dinners, then despair without a
    mouth to feed them?
Sometimes eel hollow, as if your soul would next
    collapse in shards
Without the glue of others' energies to cement your
    wholeness?

There is no cure for you, my rabid friend, save one:
    starvation,
Even that belayed with obvious risks. Yet, with God's
    caloric graces,
You may survive to live a full, productive life, though
    always
Teetering in your prayer, uneasy even in the midst of
    satisfaction,
Unable to remember dreams, in which you descend
    again to savagery.
If nothing else, you may have sterile pleasure in
    another's health.

The locked door, the telephone that does not answer,
The broken date, the promises returned empty,
Automatic siphons all, effortless for the users.
Another bite, and the tenderest spring noon is
Grayish, just more late winter, never terminating,
No time passing anymore, until death or forgetting.

They do not kiss you, and they do not kill, but extract
With every subterfuge that feeds the starving, and then more.
See how they seem to prosper, hammering out their
    bloody contracts;
Buying and selling when no volunteers turn up to alm
    with tendernesses.
It is a dangerous time again, now as they pass among us.
    Watch;
Look neither left nor right; be openhanded, but do not
    crave repayment.

And rest. In the rumored, fortunate cases, there is return
    of love.
Through we are clueless what leads to these miracles.
    Certainly, however,
There can be no cure without survival, and no survival
    without strength.
But, above all, be wary of seductions leading to surprise attack.

Be strong; be careful; be easy in forgetting pain that
    could consume you;
And never cease to keep your wait for grace, lamp ready,
    and hands open.

The War With the Angels

Can it come and take us, that hand
We picture as a wing, that shadow
Or light being? And are we not heard

As we scream, departing our undefended lives?
Is power indeed so absolute, fate so purely random?

And if it comes as a big, blond boy,
Aged 30 and 4, who will not kiss us
On the lip but gives his sandpaper
Beard instead, whom we say we love
Immensely, but who questions our facts
As if judging guilt or innocence
And then passes with our picture in hand
And another brush of beard on open lips
And may be moving closer, coming again sooner
Than the five years since his last visit.

There is some fairness in my claim I am not dying,
And he hears me, the great angel boy, and I do live.

And if they come, two flitting flecks of red,
Gone almost before they fly off through the trees,
Your little death and mine, not wanting to be spotted
And too huried, cautious, to recognize that it is I,
Smoking out on the deck, pink and prosperous of body,
And that this was, indeed, the place to spy us.

So far, I always try to talk to them. Not always that I
Wish to have them stay; never that they take me with them
To that invisibility magnificient as the sky, to clouds.
It is my defense, so now they know it: angels do not speak
Unless instructed. A soft question turns them back to find
Out what to say; thus I buy my time, conceiving against
   demise.

Be warned, stranger, whoever you may appear to be:
I go nowhere silently; when you shake my hand, I may
Wrest yours away, a cruel boy breaking the dragonfly's
    wings
Clear off, so they will not enclose and smother me,
So the heavenly bureaucracy notices only sometime later
That there is no report, that an angel is missing in the ranks.

But I am not hostile anyway, just testing my rights
Which have never seen full growth, and which, I think,
Entitle me, if I understand life's secret law and order.
And I expect no punishment, and do not fear reward.

And if it comes impersonal, as a sudden force
Against the brain, or spattering my blood; or as
A crumb within the blood itself, venous boulder
Or ravenous entity, battling to eat whatever tastes:
I may win over it again, and have before, calling
My doctors and magicians of every good persuasion,
And borrowing needed life from those who love me best.
Come and try to wrestle me; you did not conquer Jacob,
And I have long already been man of a new name
And still walk defiant, without stoop or limp
And still raise up my generations, bright for living.

I do not arrogate immortality, no, if that is not the given
For us who pass as human here in this neighborhood; I do
Not ask to be the first to live forever. I am submissive,
Everyone knows, when ordered in the proper tone and
    manner.
I am mere and weak, despite any of my forceful words.

But there is, I say, a covenant; I would enforce it.
Crumb, tell your maker that I claim my life of right,
And there are harmonies on his image still to make,
My notes against the music of these spheres, mine,
Without which the symphony would howl unresolved,
    undone.
I am needed for my singing. Will he sing my part himself?

And if it comes invisible, angel voices chanting
Which are only my own voice, and I am the reaping hand
Unknown to myself, quietly crazed toward self-destruction;
And I am infected with a pain so great that only pain
    can drive it;
Or, I am, in my own mind, incomplete and must have
    someone thinking for me:
Will I surrender then? Or will I not surrender?

Deepest of unanswerabilities. What shall I call the Death Poem?
The Milky Way. Not that. The Battle for Life, perhaps,
Chirping optimisms of the blackest color. What is the poem?
For surely there is poetry there, and just as surely hope on our
    own shore.
And none can make them coexist, unless I am the poem in
    some foreign sense,
And am found, too, immortal among the skeletons. Call the poem
Later in My Life, and write it much, much later.

Visitor or haunted, I see light in all directions—but they call
This death, and have entirely the wrong concept, the
    false term.
And I am so alive that these little, weird deaths come
    sniffing,
Growling sometimes, othertimes braying and pawing.
    Civilization encroaches.
In my dreams I am a zombie, and then I awake without
    change of state.
When would I resurrect? On what saint's birthday? In
    what new disguise?

What new set of puzzles to make labyrinthine my way?
    Death is the puzzle.
We cannot see it, only witness the passing of breath,
    cooling of meat.
How then could there be words for it; but there are too
    many words.

36

With these words I dispel you now. Hope. Faith. And
  Love's warm hand.
May we all have much of each, and of the rainbow that
  these colors make.
Light surrounds me, no different from my daylights,
  and I awaken.

Uncle Death

I read a poem once
that said death was like a rich uncle
with gold choppers
and diamond studs
who drove a big white Cadillac.

But I don't believe that.
I believe that death
is a very tall, grey eminence
whose reverence we owe.

I don't think he drives either.
Maybe he flies.
Or maybe he walks slowly like me.

I do know where he goes;
And that all of us
will follow him at some time.
That is part of the respect we owe him.
As friend, companion and healer.

AIDS House

Come on over, maybe death will be here
he works 4 days a week
sometimes visiting in the rooms
sometimes just walking around the corridors
I suppose for exercise
I suppose he likes it here

Have a seat and take off your tight shoes
so comfortable, so assuring
you could go barefoot forever

Bye

If I had a morphine pump
I'd be out of here in a half hour
So easy
Just drifting, drifting until I met
A better light
A greater joy
A new life

About the Author

Lightning Allan Brown was born in Arlington, Virginia on December 10, 1947. He grew up in Southern California, the oldest of five children, and began writing poetry as a teenager. Later, he studied and taught German Literature, and was an acclaimed teacher and scholar.

After living and studying in Europe, Lightning went to Chapel Hill, North Carolina to visit friends. He never left. Always an activist, Lightning became immersed in town politics, working for clean water and greenways, affordable housing and civil rights. He wrote a column for the local paper, frequently including his poetry, and was a recognized leader in gay rights and local government. He graduated from UNC Law School in 1990 after testing positive for HIV.

Lightning celebrated life: exploring with his dog Magic and cat Elaine, hunting for four-leaf clovers, lighting a Solstice candle each year, and cooking exotic recipes. Lightning died on February 12, 1996 surrounded by family and friends. In keeping with his wishes, his ashes were scattered in the slave's cemetery in Chapel Hill. He leaves his parents Marie and Byron Brown, sisters Susan and Nancy, and brothers Peter and Andy.